Ball Camp

by Antonio Colantoni
illustrated by Meryl Henderson

Core Decodable 43

McGraw Hill Education

Bothell, WA • Chicago, IL • Columbus, OH • New York, NY

MHEonline.com

Send all inquiries to:
McGraw-Hill Education
8787 Orion Place
Columbus, OH 43240

ISBN: 978-0-02-130445-5
MHID: 0-02-130445-9

Printed in Canada.

9 10 11 12 KOD 24

Mitch is at ball camp.

Mitch is not the best.
Mitch sits on the bench.

Beth can run fast and catch.

On the bench, Mitch and Liz clap.

Trish can bunt.
Trish got a hit.

On the bench, Mitch claps. Trish runs.

Chad can pitch.
Chad can pitch fast.

Mitch stands and claps.

Then Mitch gets to bat.
Mitch picks a thin bat.

Beth, Trish, and Chad sit on the bench.
The pitch to Mitch is fast.

Smash! Mitch hits it!

Beth, Trish, and Chad jump and clap.

Next, Mitch gets to pitch.
Beth, Trish, and Chad clap.

Mitch jumps to catch the ball!
Beth, Trish, and Chad jump and clap.

"It was fun on the bench," said Mitch.
"And it is fun to hit, pitch, and catch!"